GEORGE WASHINGTON

by Candice Ransom

Cody Koala

An Imprint of Pop!
popbooksonline.com

abdopublishing.com
Published by Pop!, a division of ABDO, PO Box 398166, Minneapolis, Minnesota 55439. Copyright © 2019 by POP, LLC. International copyrights reserved in all countries. No part of this book may be reproduced in any form without written permission from the publisher. Pop!™ is a trademark and logo of POP, LLC.

Printed in the United States of America, North Mankato, Minnesota

042018
092018

THIS BOOK CONTAINS RECYCLED MATERIALS

Cover Photo: Shutterstock Images
Interior Photos: Shutterstock Images, 1, 5, 6, 13, 16, 19 (bottom left), 19 (bottom right), 20, 21 (top left), 21 (top right); North Wind Picture Archives, 9, 21 (bottom), 11, 15, 19 (top)

Editor: Charly Haley
Series Designer: Laura Mitchell

Library of Congress Control Number: 2017963384

Publisher's Cataloging-in-Publication Data

Names: Ransom, Candice, author.
Title: George Washington / by Candice Ransom.
Description: Minneapolis, Minnesota : Pop!, 2019. | Series: Founding fathers | Includes online resources and index.
Identifiers: ISBN 9781532160226 (lib.bdg.) | ISBN 9781532161346 (ebook) |
Subjects: LCSH: Washington, George, 1732-1799--Juvenile literature. | Founding Fathers of the United States--Juvenile literature. | Statesmen --United States--Biography--Juvenile literature. | United States-- Politics and government--1783-1789--Juvenile literature.
Classification: DDC 973.4 [B]--dc23

Hello! My name is

Cody Koala

Pop open this book and you'll find QR codes like this one, loaded with information, so you can learn even more!

Scan this code* and others like it while you read, or visit the website below to make this book pop.

popbooksonline.com/george-washington

*Scanning QR codes requires a web-enabled smart device with a QR code reader app and a camera.

Table of Contents

Chapter 1

Growing Up

Young George Washington was tall and shy. He was born on a farm in Virginia. Virginia was a **colony** in America. Great Britain controlled the colonies.

Watch a video here!

George's birthplace

George learned his school lessons at home. Riding horses helped him become strong and brave.

George did not go to college.

Chapter 2

War

The colonies did not like British laws. The **American Revolutionary War** started. Washington led the American army to fight the British.

Learn more here!

The soldiers came from different colonies. They did not get along. But Washington said they were fighting together to be free. The men trusted him.

America won the war.

The colonies became the

United States.

Chapter 3

First President

A group of people wrote the **Constitution**. It had rules for the new country. It said America would have a **president**.

Complete an activity here!

Washington was already a hero. Americans chose him to be the first president of the United States. Washington helped shape the **government**.

He served as president
for eight years. Then he
went home to Mount Vernon
in Virginia. He died two
years later.

Chapter 4

America Today

Washington was a **Founding Father**. He fought for America's freedom.

Washington has been called the father of our country.

Learn more here!

He was the first president.

Other presidents follow

Washington's example.

On February 22, Washington was born in Virginia.

Washington helped create the US Constitution.

Washington returned to Virginia.

1732

1787

1797

1775–1783

1789

1799

Washington led the American troops in the war against Great Britain.

On December 14, Washington died at his home.

Washington became America's first president.

Making Connections

Text-to-Self

How is your life like Washington's life when he was young? How is it different?

Text-to-Text

Have you read another book about a person from the past? What did you learn from it?

Text-to-World

Washington was a Founding Father. How did Washington's actions shape the world you live in?

Glossary

American Revolutionary War – the war fought between the colonies and Great Britain.

colony – land ruled by another country.

Constitution – laws that explain the rights of the people and the powers of the US government.

Founding Father – one of the men who built the government of the United States.

president – a person who leads the government of a country.

Index

Online Resources

popbooksonline.com

Thanks for reading this Cody Koala book!

Scan this code* and others like it in this book, or visit the website below to make this book pop!

popbooksonline.com/george-washington

*Scanning QR codes requires a web-enabled smart device with a QR code reader app and a camera.